SOME LIKE IT HOT

ANNE INGLIS

SOME LIKE IT
H O T

WOOD ENGRAVINGS BY IAN STEPHENS

SILENT BOOKS

First published in Great Britain 1992
by Silent Books, Swavesey, Cambridge CB4 5RA

ISBN 1 85183 043 X

British Library Cataloguing-in-Publication Data.
A catalogue record for this book is available from the British
Library.

Typeset by Studio Sixteen, Over, Cambridge
Printed in Great Britain by
St Edmundsbury Press, Bury St Edmunds, Suffolk

*I*ntroduction

Hot food – you either love it or you hate it. But this integral part of the cooking of most tropical countries has now found a firm foothold on the Western eating map, witnessed by the enduring popularity of Indian restaurants in Britain, and the explosion of Malaysian, Thai, and Mexican restaurants in the US and beyond.

Finding the ingredients to re-create, say a North African or Thai meal, is now quite simple. Ethnic shops, which are usually dotted around any large city, are obvious sources, but for those living elsewhere the large supermarkets have come to the rescue with imaginative selections of herbs, vegetables, various kinds of rice and noodles, spices and flours. Unlike the complications of classical French cookery or even the demands made by much of the English tradition (good pastry, a knowledge of game) many of the ideas in *Some Like it Hot*, with their reliance on fresh vegetables and sharp flavours, can be put together quickly and eaten immediately.

It is important not to inflict unbearable hotness on either the food or on people who do not care for it. Dishes need to be seasoned creatively to bring out the best in the raw ingredients – adding spoonfuls of chilli powder just for the sake of it is a pointless way to cook and eat. Introducing heat is very much a matter of taste and personal experiment. All the recipes in *Some Like it Hot* are easily varied for more or less heat – in most cases it is a question of adding or subtracting the amount of chillis – although as they are presented the dishes are well balanced, and given their star rating accordingly. Some, such as the Pipérade or Goulash, are deliberately mild. At the other end of the scale are the Chicken 'Vindaloo', Chilli con Carne, and anything with Harissa or chilli paste (see the *chilli guide*).

A final word on seasoning: chillis, with their natural spice, require the addition of less salt for flavour – but salt is still crucial to a dish tasting its best and can magically highlight existing flavours.

Chilli Guide

Chillis, such a wonderful source of instant southern heat, should always be treated with respect. No matter how hot you like your food, a little chilli goes a long way, and it is wise to err on the side of caution. Sources of heat are in the seeds and the white membranes inside the pod – these should be removed for milder flavours. Always wear gloves, or at least be aware of the fierceness of the heat, since rubbing your eyes after touching chillis, either fresh or dried, can be extremely painful, especially for wearers of contact lenses.

Choosing chillis can be a confusing business. First, there is the choice between green and red, and second between dried and fresh. As with many vegetables, green is a sign of youth, and red of maturity, and as with sweet green and red peppers the green chilli is often far stronger than the red. For hot fresh peppers, try and find the small, narrow, and intensely hot Thai peppers or the equally hot and very pretty squat red, yellow, and green chillis known as the Scots Bonnet, the kind most used in the Caribbean. The most reliable sources for these are West Indian, Thai, or Indian shops. At the other end of the scale are the medium-sized European red and green chillis, the variety generally available in most shops and supermarkets, and often disappointingly mild and flavourless – sometimes only a little stronger than the larger sweet pepper.

Dried red chillis are reliably strong. Whole dried chillis need soaking before being used in sauces such as Harissa (see p 15), but they may be put dried, with seeds, into dishes where chilli is a flavouring (rather like a bay leaf) and not designed to be eaten. For simple, ready-made chilli flavouring there are the powders such as cayenne pepper – ground dried cayenne peppers – or chilli powder, which is a blend of spices with dried chilli as a base. In the UK, where finding hot chillis can be a hit or miss affair, to create a truly fiery flavour in a dish it is probably safest to choose dried chillis, which are versatile and the most reliable. Chilli powder may be used either as an alternative or as a powerful way of strengthening heat.

The chilli, so often used in the traditional Indian restaurant curry, in fact has its origins far away in the Americas, where it was grown by the Indians and much prized as a flavouring which dispensed with the necessity to use much salt. Recent research has shown that excessive consumption of chilli, curries, and generally hot food can lead to addiction – capsaicin, the substance in the seeds and white veins, stimulates the release of endorphins, the body's natural painkillers. Not surprising, then, that chilli is now the most consumed spice in the world. It has indeed travelled a long way since its cultivated beginnings by the American Indians first intrigued Columbus and the early settlers.

Spice Guide

Most of the ingredients asked for in recipes from India, Malaysia, Thailand, and other countries with a fondness for spicy food, are now easy to track down. Dried spices as relatively familiar as cumin, coriander, and cardamom now take their place alongside many fresh ingredients such as lemon grass, ginger, and even fresh turmeric – a tuber, rather like fresh ginger. Spices should always be stored carefully in airtight containers, and used as freshly as possible – taste fades quickly, and stale spices do little to enhance a dish. This glossary highlights the ingredients in *Some Like it Hot*, and is not intended to be a comprehensive list of all available herbs and spices.

Caraway

A sweet, aniseed-related seed, shaped like a half moon. Aside from its main uses in breads such as pumpernickel, it is an important element in several North African dishes.

Cardamom

Related to the ginger family, the most widely available cardamom is usually the green pod variety. Sometimes the pod is used whole for flavouring, elsewhere it is the fragrant black seeds inside which flavour a dish.

Coriander

A versatile plant with seeds and pungent fresh leaves. The two elements are not interchangeable: use the leaves for salads and garnishes, and the seeds – roasted whole, roasted then ground, or simply ground – as a spice.

Cumin

Small pale brown seeds which are often roasted to give an additionally nutty flavour – an essential ingredient of Indian cookery.

Fennel

A sweet seed, with an aniseed-like taste. The leaves of the plant are often used to flavour fish.

Garam Masala

A combination of several spices used to flavour Indian food. This may be bought ready made, or put together as follows:

> 1 tbsp cardamom seeds
> 1 heaped tsp ground cinnamon
> 1 tsp black peppercorns
> 1 tsp cumin seeds
> 1 tsp ground cloves
> 1 tsp nutmeg

Grind together in a pepper mill or coffee grinder, and store in an airtight container.

Ginger

In its fresh form this is a fibrous tuber, which needs peeling and chopping (or grating) very finely. There is also a powdered form, normally used in cakes.

Lemon Grass

A typically Thai ingredient with an intense lemony flavour. The dry stem needs soaking before using, though the fresh version is now more readily available.

Mustard

An important spice, especially in cooking of North America and Europe. Use ready made, or for English mustard mix your own for freshness. Mustard seeds, usually fried to sweeten the taste, are used in curries.

Turmeric

A yellow spice, used for colour and flavour. Usually sold as a finely ground powder, it is now occasionally available in its fresh tuber form.

Recipes

A very hot chilli paste found in North African cooking. Eaten with couscous, when it is usually diluted
with water, it is also a useful way of enlivening any
dish where extra heat is liked.

> 4 oz (125 g) dried red chillis
> 2 fat cloves garlic, peeled
> 2 tbsp water
> 1 heaped tsp coriander, ground
> ½ tsp caraway seed, ground
> 1 heaped tsp salt

Cut the chillis open, remove the seeds, leave to soak in plenty
of water for 20 minutes, and then drain. Place the chillis, garlic
cloves and water in a liquidiser, blend thoroughly, and gently
add the spices and salt, mixing well. Put into a bowl or jar and
store, covered well, in the fridge or cool larder.

This is a concentrated plain pepper mixture, without extra spices, used in much of the southeast Asian cookery of Thailand and Vietnam, and serviceable elsewhere where red chillis are required. Serve sparingly.

> 2 oz (60 g) dried red chillis
> 2 cloves garlic
> Juice and finely grated rind of 1 lime
> Salt
> 1 heaped tsp sugar

Deseed the chillis, and soak for 20 minutes in a bowl of water. Drain, keeping some of the liquid to moisten the paste. Blend the chillis with the garlic, and spoon the mixture into a bowl, adding the lime juice and rind, and the reserved water. Season well with salt and sugar. Cover and store in the fridge or freezer.

Piri-Piri Sauce

I first tried this fiery sauce in the Lisbon restaurant Bomjardim. Chicken are basted in the sauce, then roasted on spits in the street outside. Each bird arrives at table sitting regally on a huge nest of chips, and accompanied by a little pot of piri-piri which is presented with a small brush for the customer to paint on extra heat, if liked.

6 dried red chillis
Olive oil

Leave the chillis with their seeds and stalks and place in the bottom of a clean jam jar or similar storage pot. Fill to the top with oil – the chillis should take up about a quarter of the jar – stir briefly, close tightly, and leave to infuse for a fortnight before using. Piri-piri is also excellent for enlivening plain pasta – a few drops are enough.

Rouille

A French peppery mayonnaise which, spread on croûtons, is the traditional accompaniment for bouillabaisse or fish soup.

2 – 3 garlic cloves
2 fresh red chillis, deseeded and chopped
Salt
2 egg yolks
8 fl oz (250 ml) olive oil
Black pepper
Cayenne

Blend the garlic, chillis, and a good pinch of salt together to make a thick purée. Stir in the egg yolks, then add the olive oil drop by drop, exactly as making mayonnaise. Season with black pepper and cayenne.

A spicy dip, perfect for fish or shellfish, and a good alternative to straight mayonnaise.

2 egg yolks
1 tbsp wholegrain or English (made-up) mustard
3 oz (75 g) prawns, cooked
8 fl oz (250 ml) groundnut or olive oil
2 tbsp shallots or spring onions, finely chopped
Lemon juice
Salt and black pepper
Tabasco

In a blender whisk together the egg yolks, mustard and prawns, making a smooth purée. Add the oil drop by drop, in the same manner as making mayonnaise, progressing slowly until the mixture begins to thicken. Fold in the shallots and season with lemon juice, salt, pepper, and Tabasco.

A spicy vinegar to give extra kick to salads and dressings.

> 6 green chillis
> 1 shallot, finely chopped
> 1 pint (550 ml) cider vinegar

If preferred, deseed the chillis first (far less heat), otherwise roughly cut into smallish pieces and place in a bottle with the chopped shallot. In a pan bring the vinegar to the boil and pour over the chilli and shallot mixture. Leave to cool and cover. Allow a month before using when the vinegar should be strained.

Mint and Coconut Chutney

A spicy fresh-tasting chutney which is an excellent accompaniment for plainly cooked fish or meat.

1 fresh red chilli, deseeded and finely chopped
2 oz (60 g) dried shredded coconut
1 – 2 tbsp lime juice
1 big handful fresh mint
2 tbsp water
3 tbsp plain yoghurt
Grated rind of 1 lemon
Salt

In a food processor mix together the chilli, coconut, lime juice, mint, water, and yoghurt to make a coarse purée. Add the lemon rind and season with salt to taste. Store in a small container, well covered, in the fridge.

Fresh Tomato 'Chutney'

Very easy to make, this thick sauce is a good side dish as well as an even-tempered accompaniment to most curries.

1 tsp cumin seeds
1 tsp coriander seeds
4 small tomatoes, peeled,
   deseeded, and diced
1 inch (2.5 cm) fresh ginger, peeled, and
   grated
1 large fresh red chilli,
   deseeded, and finely chopped
1 squeeze lime juice
1 tsp grated rind of 1 lime
1 tbsp olive oil
2 tbsp fresh coriander
2 tbsp natural yoghurt
Salt

Heat a small, non-stick frying pan, and cook the cumin seeds until they turn a golden brown. Remove, and with the coriander seeds roughly crush in a mortar or spice grinder. In a bowl, mix the crushed seeds with the tomatoes, ginger and chilli. Leave half an hour and drain. Now add the lime juice, grated lime rind, olive oil, coriander, and yoghurt, and season with salt. Chill before serving. To keep, store well covered in the fridge.

This excellent Mexican avocado dip achieved high fashion during the dinner parties of the 1970s. It deserves to be rehabilitated quickly.

> 2 tbsp spring onions, finely chopped
> 2 fresh green chillis, deseeded and finely chopped
> 2 tbsp fresh coriander, chopped – or more to taste
> Salt
> 2 ripe avocados
> 1 large tomato, peeled, deseeded and chopped

In a blender mix together the spring onions, chillis, coriander and salt until you have made a rough purée. Separately, cut open the avocados, remove the stone and mash the contents. Mix in the purée and add the chopped tomato. Check the seasoning.

Salsas – hot and spicy Southern American and Mexican sauces – are a wonderfully versatile way of enlivening eggs, fish, meat, tortillas, tacos, seafood ... Combinations are endless. This one is unusual and pretty.

> 2 sweet red peppers
> 3 slices of 1 small pineapple, cored, and finely chopped
> 1 green chilli, deseeded and diced
> 3 spring onions, finely chopped
> 2 tbsp fresh mint, finely chopped
> Juice of 1 lime
> Salt and black pepper
> 1 tsp sugar, or to taste

Roast the red peppers over a flame on top of the gas stove, or cook under the grill, until the skins are blackened and the flesh soft. Cool, deseed, and chop finely. Add the pepper to the rest of the ingredients, and season.

A hot Spanish sauce, much in the same tradition as harissa or other chilli-based sauces, though not as fiery. It is intended to be eaten with shellfish.

4 tbsp olive oil
1 medium onion, finely chopped
4 garlic cloves, finely chopped
1 large tomato, peeled, deseeded and chopped
1 sweet red pepper, roasted, the skin and seeds removed, and chopped
2 dried red chillis, deseeded and roughly chopped
2 tbsp water
2 tbsp white wine
1 oz (25 g) almonds, lightly toasted
Salt

In a pan heat half the olive oil and sweat the onion and garlic until golden. Add the tomato, pepper, chillis, water and wine. Simmer for 20 minutes. In a blender process the almonds, then add the tomato and chilli mixture and the remaining olive oil, adding more if necessary for a smooth sauce. Season with salt.

*H*ot and Sour Soup

Serves 6

Variations on the hot and sour theme occur any-
where from Vietnam and Malaysia to the spicy
Szechuan cooking of China. This recipe has a
Thai emphasis.

> 2 pints (1.1 l) chicken stock
> 1 tsp chilli paste
> 2 chicken breasts, skinned, and diced
> 3 stalks lemon grass, white bulb part only,
>   finely sliced (optional)
> 3 spring onions, finely chopped
> 3 green chillis, deseeded and finely sliced
> 4 oz (125 g) fresh prawns, shelled and
>   deveined
> 4 tbsp Nam Pla (fish sauce – available from
>   Thai or Chinese shops)
> Juice of 2 limes
> Salt
> 1 oz (25 g) fresh coriander, chopped

Put half the stock into a large saucepan and bring to the boil.
Add the chilli paste, and blend well with the back of a wooden
spoon. Turn down the stove, and add the chicken, lemon
grass, spring onions and chillis, simmering for about 10
minutes, then pouring in the rest of the stock with the prawns.
Return to the boil, and finish with the fish sauce and lime juice.
Season well with salt, and sprinkle with coriander.

Gazpacho

Serves 6

A rich soup from Andalucia, Spain, wonderful for quenching thirst on a scorching summer's day. The addition of chilli makes the soup more fiery than it is sometimes served, but the ultimate effect is even more cooling.

4 garlic cloves
Salt
5 oz (150 g) fresh brown breadcrumbs
6 tbsp olive oil
1 tbsp lemon juice
1 tbsp red wine vinegar
Black pepper, freshly ground
1 lb (500 g) tomatoes, skinned, deseeded, and chopped
3 green chillis, deseeded and chopped
1 small cucumber, chopped
1 red pepper, deseeded and coarsely chopped
1 medium onion, peeled and quartered
10 fl oz (275 ml) tomato juice
8 oz (250 g) crushed ice

Pound the garlic with a little salt to make a paste. Stir in the breadcrumbs and mix well, then add the olive oil, drop by drop. Season with lemon juice, vinegar, and salt and pepper and set aside. Put the tomatoes in a blender with the chillis, cucumber, red pepper and onion, and blend for about 15 seconds to a roughish texture. Mix the vegetables and the garlic and breadcrumb paste, and add the tomato juice. Correct the seasoning. Finally, add the ice, and mix well.

*C*urried Fresh Pea Soup

Serves 4

This mildly curried soup may be eaten hot, at room temperature, and works well chilled too.

1 oz (25 g) butter
1 small onion, finely chopped
½ medium carrot, diced
½ stick celery, finely diced
1 clove garlic, finely chopped
½ tsp curry powder
6 oz (175 g) fresh peas, shelled weight
1½ pints (825 ml) chicken stock
2 tbsp natural yoghurt
Salt

Melt the butter in a large frying pan, and sweat the onion, carrot, celery and garlic for 5 – 10 minutes, until the vegetables have lost their 'crunch'. Add the curry powder, stir for about 30 seconds, mix in the peas and pour on the boiling stock. Bring to the boil and then simmer for 15 minutes. In the blender purée the mixture. Taste for seasoning and add the yoghurt.

Serves 4

A spicy North African soup which is very easy to make. This version is a variation from Sousse in Tunisia.

> 1 tsp harissa (see p 15)
> 1 garlic clove, finely chopped
> ½ tsp ground cumin
> 2 tbsp olive oil
> 1½ pints (825 ml) water
> 3 oz (75 g) couscous grains
> 1 egg
> Salt

Mix the harissa with the garlic and the ground cumin. In a large saucepan heat the oil, and add, first the harissa mixture, then the water. Bring to the boil, add the couscous, and simmer for 15 minutes. Just before serving break in the egg, mixing in the yolk and white to create a shredded effect. Correct the seasoning with salt.

Cucumber Salad

Serves 4 as a side salad

A refreshing, unusual salad, variations of which are found anywhere from the Caribbean to Thailand. The green vegetables speckled with the bright red chilli look very pretty.

> 1 medium cucumber
> 2 courgettes, coarsely grated
> Salt
> 1 large clove garlic, finely chopped
> Grated rind and juice of 1 lime
> 1 fresh red chilli, deseeded and finely
>   chopped
> 1 tbsp coriander, chopped
> Sugar
> Black pepper

Peel the cucumbers, cut lengthways, and remove the seeds. Dice, place in a bowl with the grated courgette, sprinkle with salt, and leave half an hour. Rinse under running water and drain thoroughly, squeezing the juice out with your hands. Place in a serving bowl with the garlic, lime rind and juice, the chopped chilli, and coriander, and season with sugar and black pepper to taste.

Grilled Salad

Serves 4

A dish typical of many found in Tunisia and elsewhere in North Africa. It is often eaten without the addition of chilli, but when added the amount can be unpredictable ...

> 2 large red sweet peppers
> 3 – 4 large ripe tomatoes
> 2 fresh red chillis
> 5 – 6 spring onions, chopped
> 2 tbsp parsley, chopped
> 1 tbsp mint, chopped
> Juice of 1 lemon
> 3 tbsp olive oil
> Salt and black pepper

Cook the peppers and chillis, either over a flame or under the grill, or roasted in a hot oven. When ready the skins should look peeling and burned, and the flesh soft to the touch. The tomatoes may be prepared in the same way, or simply peeled, deseeded, and chopped. Cool the vegetables in a paper bag until the skins become loose. Peel and deseed the vegetables, chop finely and place in a serving bowl. Add the spring onions, parsley, mint, lemon juice and olive oil, season and mix well.

Beef, Garlic, and Chilli Salad

Serves 4

A quick and traditional Thai dish. The European milder green chilli works well in this dish – four Thai chillis make an extremely hot salad.

> 3 tbsp vegetable or groundnut oil
> 12 oz (350 g) beef fillet, sliced very thinly
> 4 – 5 garlic cloves
> Salt
> 1 inch (2.5 cm) fresh ginger, peeled, and
>   finely chopped
> 1 tbsp soya sauce
> 3 tbsp lime juice
> 3 spring onions, finely chopped
> 4 green chillis, deseeded and finely sliced
> Sugar
> Fresh coriander, finely chopped

Heat the oil in a frying pan, and sear the beef until just browned on both sides. Remove and set aside. Pound the garlic to a paste with a little salt, and mix with the ginger, soya sauce, and lime juice. Add the spring onions and chillis, and season to taste with sugar and black pepper. Turn the beef strips in the dressing, making sure each is well coated, and serve sprinkled with coriander.

Serves 4

A deliciously simple and rightly popular Italian dish which originates in Rome.

    1 lb (500 g) spaghetti
    8 tbsp olive oil
    4 garlic cloves, finely chopped
    1 dried red chilli
    Salt and black pepper

Bring a large pan of salted water to the boil, and cook the spaghetti in the usual way. In a frying pan heat the olive oil, and sauté the garlic and whole chilli until the garlic is golden brown. Drain the spaghetti and toss into the frying pan, making sure the garlic and chilli mixture coats the strands of pasta. Correct the seasoning with salt and black pepper.

Pasta alla Puttanesca

Serves 4

A grittily named pasta dish (puttanesca means prostitute) which is supremely popular in Italy.

3 tbsp olive oil
3 garlic cloves, finely chopped
1 dried red chilli, deseeded and crumbled
1 14 oz (400 g) tin chopped tomatoes
1 tbsp tomato purée
2 oz (60 g) tin anchovies
4 oz (125 g) black olives, pitted and halved
2 tbsp capers
Salt and black pepper
12 oz (350 g) spaghetti
Plenty of chopped basil or parsley

In a pan heat the oil and cook the garlic until golden, then add the chilli, tomatoes, tomato purée, anchovies, olives and capers. Simmer for 30 minutes until you have a thick but still liquid sauce. Now bring a large pan of salted water to the boil, and cook the spaghetti in the usual way. Drain, and in a large bowl mix in the sauce. Taste, season, and sprinkle with the basil or parsley.

Red Couscous

Serves 6-8

Easy to prepare, this colourful couscous can be
served with a main dish such as lamb stew or as a
spicy alternative to potatoes.

  8 oz (250 g) couscous
  3 tbsp vegetable oil
  3 garlic cloves, finely chopped
  2 tsp harissa (see p 19), diluted with a little water
  2 tbsp tomato purée
  1 tsp ground caraway
  Salt

Soak the couscous grains in warm water for 30 minutes, running your hands through the grains every few minutes so they
remain separated. Steam the soaked couscous over a pan of
boiling water for about 20 minutes. Meanwhile, heat the oil in
a large pan and stir in the garlic, diluted harissa, tomato purée
and caraway. Cover and simmer for five minutes. Add a few
spoonfuls of water to moisten the sauce, and mix it into the
couscous. Correct the seasoning with salt.

There are many variants on the theme of Boston Baked Beans, including the tinned variety known to every child. This recipe, a far cry from beans on toast, uses bacon for extra flavouring as well as some hottish spices.

1 lb (500 g) haricot beans
2 bay leaves
2 medium onions, roughly chopped
2 tbsp black treacle
1 tbsp English mustard powder
½ tsp mustard seeds
2 tbsp fresh oregano, chopped
8 oz (250 g) smoked slab bacon
¼ pint (140 ml) tomato juice
Dash of Tabasco
½ tsp chilli powder
Black pepper

Soak the beans overnight. Bring them to the boil in plenty of water with the bay leaves, boil for 10 minutes, then drain. Pre-heat the oven to Gas Mark 2 (300°F, 150°C). Take a large casserole dish and place half the beans at the bottom with the onions, treacle, mustard powder, mustard seeds and oregano. Cut the bacon with a criss-cross pattern and place on top of the beans. Seal the bacon with the second half of the beans, and pour on the tomato juice mixed with the Tabasco and chilli powder. Barely cover with boiling water, and simmer in the oven for a minimum of 4 hours, making sure every now and then that there is enough liquid to keep the dish moist. For a crusty top remove the lid for the last hour of cooking.

Green Chilli Fry-up

Serves 4

A summer dish, typical of home cooking in the American Southwest region. For a more substantial dish add slices of cooked chorizo sausage, though the true authenticity of this is doubtful.

> 8 mild green European chillis
> 4 cobs of corn
> 1 medium onion, finely chopped
> 4 tbsp light vegetable oil
> 3 tomatoes, peeled, deseeded and chopped
> 3 courgettes or different squash, diced
> 2 chorizo sausages, cooked and sliced
>   (optional)
> 1 tbsp fresh oregano, finely chopped
> 3 tbsp coriander, finely chopped
> Salt and black pepper

Roast the chillis in the oven or grill over an open flame. Leave to cool in a paper bag, then cut open, deseed, and chop finely. Cut the kernels off the corn cobs with a sharp knife and set aside. Heat the oil in a wide, deep frying pan and add the onion. Sweat for a few minutes until golden, then add the chillis, corn, tomatoes, courgettes, and chorizo (if used). Heat through until the vegetables are cooked but still crunchy, season well with the herbs and salt and pepper, and serve hot or cold.

Serves 6

From India, a deliciously fragrant way to eat some
of our northern vegetables.

2 green peppers
1 small cauliflower
1 head of broccoli
4 small potatoes
6 tbsp vegetable oil
2 tsp cumin
2 tbsp ground coriander
1 tsp turmeric
1 green chilli, deseeded, and finely
    chopped
1 dried red chilli, deseeded, and flaked
1 14 oz (400 g) tin chopped tomatoes
15 fl oz (450 ml) boiling water
2 tsp sea salt
Grated rind of half a lemon
Fresh coriander, chopped

Slice the peppers into long strips, cut the cauliflower in florets,
and slice the potato into fat pieces. Heat the oil in a large frying
pan, and add the cumin seeds for a few seconds until they turn
brown. Stir in the coriander, turmeric, and green chilli, and
chilli flakes with the prepared vegetables. Cook for about five
minutes, then add the tomatoes, and cook over a high heat for
another five minutes. Add the boiling water and the salt, and
simmer a quarter of an hour. Sprinkle with fresh coriander.

Pipérade

Serves 2 – 3

A delicious combination of sweet peppers and eggs, enlivened with chilli, from the Basque regions of France and Spain. This can be accompanied for a light lunch or supper by a simply dressed green salad.

3 large red peppers
1 large fresh chilli
3 tbsp olive oil
1 large onion, finely chopped
1 large clove garlic, finely chopped
4 large tomatoes, peeled, deseeded, and chopped
1 tbsp thyme, finely chopped
1 bay leaf
6 eggs
2 tbsp parsley, chopped
Salt

Either roast in the oven or grill the peppers and the chilli over a naked flame so the skin becomes blackened and the flesh soft to the touch. Leave to cool in a paper bag. Skin the vegetables, then deseed and slice them into fine strips. Heat the oil in a frying pan, add the onion, garlic, the peppers and chilli, the tomatoes, thyme and the bay leaf. Season with salt, and sweat gently for five minutes. In a bowl beat the eggs with the chopped parsley, and then add to the pepper mixture in the pan, stirring gently until the texture of scrambled eggs is reached.

Serves 6

This is a pie for all those who like a tangy but mild heat in their food, but no less delicious for its gentleness.

10 oz (275 g) plain flour, sifted
6 tsp English mustard, freshly made
Salt and black pepper
5 oz (150 g) salted butter
4 oz (125 g) Gruyère cheese, finely grated
1 tbsp thyme, finely chopped
1 lb 8 oz (675 g) pork sausage meat
2 medium eggs, hard-boiled, peeled and sliced
4 small tomatoes, peeled and sliced
Beaten egg to glaze

Preheat oven to Gas Mark 5 (375°F, 190°C), and grease a round, shallow 7″/18 cm pie/cake tin. In a large bowl, work together the flour and half the prepared mustard, and season. Cut the butter into small pieces and knead into the flour until the mixture resembles fine breadcrumbs. Add the cheese, and about 5 tbsp water to make a smooth dough. Chill for an hour. In another bowl mix the sausage meat with the remaining mustard, thyme, salt and pepper. Now roll out two-thirds of the dough into a circle and line the bottom and sides of the tin. Take half the sausage mixture and press down on to the dough. Use half the eggs and tomatoes to form the next layer. Season well. Repeat with another layer of sausage, and a layer of tomatoes and eggs, again seasoning well, Roll out the remaining pastry to make a lid, seal the edges well with a little water, and pierce with two small air vents. Brush with beaten egg and bake for 50 minutes.

*T*una Ceviche

Serves 4

The idea of marinading raw fish is found along the coast from California through to South America. This version with tuna is simple and pretty. Any sort of white fish may be substituted – the fish should be very fresh. Eat this with a salad or on its own as a first course.

Juice of 3 lemons
Juice of 3 limes
1 tbsp fresh ginger, peeled and grated
1 fresh red chilli, deseeded and finely chopped
3 – 4 spring onions, finely chopped
1 tbsp coarse salt
1 lb 4 oz (600 g) fresh tuna
Half a sweet red pepper, finely diced
2 tbsp olive oil
2 tbsp coriander, finely chopped
Grated rind of 1 lime

In a large glass bowl mix together the lemon and lime juice, ginger, chilli, spring onions and salt. Take the tuna, wipe clean with a damp cloth, remove bones and skin, if any, and carefully cut into small, ½″ (1 cm) cubes with a sharp knife. Add the tuna to the marinade, turn to make sure every surface is wet, and leave covered in the fridge for 2 – 3 hours, placing at room temperature about 20 minutes before serving. Add the red pepper, olive oil, coriander and lime zest, mix well, and if necessary correct the seasoning with salt.

Serves 6 – 8

A wonderful dish where the texture of the salt cod resists disintegrating into a pulp, and the residual salt of the fish adds to the spicy flavour of this colourful 'stew'. Serve with boiled potatoes or rice, plainly boiled.

3 lb (1.4 kg) salt cod
2 tbsp vegetable or olive oil
1 large onion, finely chopped
1 small carrot, diced
1 stick of celery, diced
2 14 oz (400 g) tins chopped tomatoes
3 garlic cloves, finely chopped
1 sweet yellow pepper, diced
1 sweet red pepper, diced
1 bay leaf
2 parsley stalks
1 tbsp fresh thyme, chopped
1 inch (2.5 cm) cube of fresh ginger,
    peeled and grated
3 – 4 green or red fresh chillis, deseeded
    and chopped
Salt and black pepper
3 tbsp coriander, chopped

Soak the cod in plenty of cold water for at least 48 hours, changing the water morning and evening. Wash the fish, put into a pan, and cover with either water or milk. Bring to the boil, and then simmer for about eight minutes. Leave to cool, then flake into just larger than bite-size pieces, removing the bones and skin. In a large frying pan heat the oil, and sweat the onion, carrot and celery for five minutes. Add the tomatoes, the garlic, yellow and red peppers, bay leaf, parsley, thyme, ginger and chillis. Cook down until the sauce has thickened. Taste, and season with black pepper. Remove the bay leaf and parsley. Add the salt cod, and mix well, taste again, and if necessary add salt. Sprinkle with fresh coriander.

Serves 4

A West Indian curry where the addition of fresh lime juice helps offset the heat of the spices. Serve with plenty of boiled rice.

> 3 tbsp vegetable oil
> 1 large onion, finely chopped
> 2 tsp chilli paste (see p 16)
> 1 garlic clove, crushed
> 1 tbsp fresh ginger, peeled and finely chopped
> 2 tsp ground coriander
> 1 tsp ground cumin
> 2 tsp black mustard seeds, ground
> Black pepper
> 1 14 oz (400 g) tin tomatoes, drained and chopped
> Juice of 1 lime
> 2 bay leaves
> Salt
> 1 lb (500 g) medium raw prawns, peeled and deveined

In a large frying pan heat the oil and fry the onions until golden. Add the chilli paste, garlic, ginger, coriander, cumin, mustard seeds and several twists of black pepper, stir to mix. Now put in the tomatoes, lime juice, bay leaves, and season with salt, simmering for about half an hour. Five minutes before serving add the prawns, and cover for a few minutes until cooked through but not overcooked.

Serves 4

Substitute chicken, beef or pork for the prawns if
liked – all are authentic.

3 – 4 oz (125 g) egg noodles
1 tsp chilli paste
1 tsp turmeric
½ tsp anchovy paste
1 tsp cider vinegar
10 fl oz (275 ml) coconut milk
8 oz (250 g) shelled prawns
2 oz (60 g) peas
Half a small onion, roughly chopped

Bring plenty of salted water to the boil and cook the noodles
until just tender. Drain and set aside. Mix the chilli paste,
turmeric, anchovy paste and cider vinegar together. In another
pan heat the coconut milk, and add the chilli mixture, making
sure it is well blended. Now add 10 fl oz (275 ml) boiling water
to thin down the texture to a soup consistency, simmer, and
add the prawns, peas, chopped onion, and noodles. Season
well with salt. Cook over a low heat for five minutes and
serve immediately.

Serves 6

A portable dish, with a curry dip using a mayonnaise formula.

> Flour, seasoned with salt and pepper
> 12 chicken drumsticks
> 1 egg, beaten
> Vegetable oil
> 2 tbsp sesame seeds
>
> *Curry dip*
> 2 egg yolks
> Juice of half a lemon
> 7 fl oz (195 ml) sunflower or peanut oil
> 3 fl oz (80 ml) light sesame oil
> 2 tsp curry powder (or more if liked)
> 1 tsp mango chutney
> Salt and black pepper

Spread the seasoned flour on a large plate, and dip each drumstick in beaten egg then flour. Pour 1 " (2.5 cm) oil into a frying pan, heat until just smoking, and drop in the drumsticks. Cook until golden brown and crispy, remove from the oil, and drain on absorbent paper. Roast the sesame seeds under the grill, and sprinkle over the chicken. *Curry dip*: whisk the egg yolks with the lemon juice, and gradually beat in the olive oil, drop by drop, until the mayonnaise thickens. Season with the curry powder, chutney, and salt and pepper.

Chicken 'Vindaloo'

Serves 4

This Indian curry is for all those Vindaloo enthusiasts who want to go some way towards re-creating the taste of their local takeaway.

6 oz (175 g) onions, finely chopped
4 oz (125 g) shallots, finely chopped
6 garlic cloves, finely chopped
1 inch (2.5 cm) fresh ginger, peeled and grated
2 tbsp ground coriander
1 tbsp ground fennel seeds
1 tbsp ground cumin
1 14 oz (400 g) tin chopped tomatoes
4 tbsp vegetable oil
1 tsp turmeric
3 dried red chillis, deseeded, soaked for 30 minutes, then chopped
OR 1 tsp chilli paste (see p 20)
½ tsp paprika
4 chicken breasts, boned and skinned
2 tsp chilli powder
Salt
Fresh coriander, chopped

In a saucepan place the onions, shallots, garlic, ginger, coriander, fennel, and cumin, adding 15 fl oz (450 ml) water. Boil for 20 minutes. Add the tomatoes, mix well, and cook another 10 minutes over moderate heat. In a separate frying pan heat the oil, and mix in the turmeric, the crumbled chillis, and the paprika. Add the chicken, the chilli powder, and the onion mixture. Bring to the boil, and then simmer until the meat is cooked, (10 – 15 minutes). Check the seasoning, and sprinkle with coriander.

Chilli Con Carne

Serves 6

A classic Texan and Southwestern American dish
which started life in the early 19th century as a way
of making a little meat go a long way with generous
additions of chilli. Here the fiery heat is added with
mashed chillis instead of the lazier chilli powder.
Serve with rice or the more usual cooked kidney
beans.

2 lb (900 g) stewing steak
1 lb (450 g) boneless pork
3 tbsp lard or bacon fat
1 large onion, finely chopped
5 cloves garlic, finely chopped
8 dried red chillis, soaked for half an hour
   in water, deseeded, and blended with a
   little of the water to make a pulp OR
   2 tsp chilli paste (see p 16)
2 14 oz (400 g) tins Italian plum tomatoes,
   chopped
1 pint (550 ml) beef stock
1 tbsp fresh oregano, finely chopped
1 tsp ground cumin
2 bay leaves
Salt and black pepper
Cayenne pepper
Chopped fresh red chilli for garnish

Cut beef and pork into 1″ (2.5 cm) pieces. Melt the fat in a large saucepan, and brown the meat until it is well sealed on both sides. Remove with a slotted spoon, and replace with the onions and garlic, which should sweat until golden. Add the browned beef and pork, chilli pulp or paste, chopped tomatoes, beef stock, oregano, cumin and bay leaves, and simmer over an extremely low heat for about two hours, or until the meat is tender. Taste, correct the seasoning with salt and pepper, add cayenne pepper for more heat if liked, and garnish with the red chilli.

Serves 6

This national Hungarian dish comes in all sorts of forms from a thin soup to a thick stew. This version, a thinnish stew, is considered the most authentic.

 1 tbsp lard or vegetable oil
 2 medium onions, finely chopped
 1 tsp caraway seeds, ground in a mortar
 1 lb (500 g) stewing steak, cut into 1″ (2.5 cm) pieces
 2 parsley stalks
 2 sweet red peppers, finely sliced
 1 large tomato, skinned, deseeded, and roughly chopped
 1 clove garlic, crushed
 1 tsp paprika
 Salt
 2 pints (1.1 l) beef stock
 1 lb (500 g) potatoes, diced

In a large casserole melt the lard and gently fry the onion until golden. Remove the onion, raise heat, and replace with the beef which should be nicely browned, using more lard if necessary. Sprinkle the ground caraway into the pan, and add the cooked onion, the parsley stalks, peppers, tomato, garlic, cayenne, and a large pinch of salt, and cover with some of the beef stock. As the stew becomes thicker gradually add the rest of the stock, lower the heat, and simmer for about two hours. About half an hour before serving add the potatoes, and simmer until cooked. Check the seasoning and remove the parsley stalks.

Lamb with Spinach

Serves 6

A wonderful combination, liked not only in India where they enhance the flavours with spices as in this recipe, but also in Greece where the meat is softened with lemon juice. The dish is medium hot, so add more chilli powder if preferred.

1 tbsp garam masala
5 oz (150 g) natural yoghurt
2 lb (1 kg) spinach, washed and finely chopped
6 tbsp vegetable oil
1 lb 8 oz (750 g) lean lamb, cubed
1 tsp ground coriander
6 shallots, finely chopped
2 inch (5 cm) fresh ginger, peeled and diced
2 tsp turmeric
2 green chillis
1 tsp chilli powder
1 tbsp mustard seed
4 garlic cloves, mashed to a paste with a little warm water
Salt

Marinade the lamb in the garam masala and the yoghurt, and leave overnight. The next day heat the oil in a large frying-pan, and add the lamb and the coriander, cooking over a high heat until the meat is well browned and the marinade juices cooked down. Stir in the shallots, ginger, turmeric, and chillis, and fry together for a minute. Now add the chilli powder, mustard seeds and the garlic, and place the spinach on top. Cover, and cook at a high heat for about a minute. Now mix all the ingredients together well, adding water if the texture is too dry. Cover, and cook for about 40 minutes, until the meat is tender and the liquid evaporated. Correct the seasoning with salt.

A bread from the American South, quick and easy to make as no yeast is required.

2 eggs, size 3
5 fl oz (150 ml) vegetable oil
8 fl oz (225 ml) sour cream
5 oz (150 g) cornmeal
1 tsp salt
1 tbsp baking powder
Kernels of one corn cob, grated
4 large and mild green chillis, deseeded
    and finely chopped
5 oz (150 g) strong Cheddar cheese, grated

Heavily oil and line a 12″ x 8″ (30 cm x 20 cm) baking tin and preheat the oven to Gas Mark 7 (425°F, 220°C). In a bowl mix the eggs, oil, sour cream, cornmeal and salt. Sieve in the baking powder. Add the grated corn kernels, the chillis and half the Cheddar. Spread the mixture in the prepared tin and sprinkle with the rest of the cheese. Bake for 20 – 25 minutes, until a tester comes out cleanly.

An unusual recipe for strawberries using balsamic vinegar – a well-matured, concentrated vinegar of which the best examples come from Modena in northern Italy.

For each person take:
4 oz (125 g) strawberries
1 tbsp balsamic vinegar
Black pepper
1 tbsp brown sugar
2 tbsp crême fraîche

Hull and halve the strawberries. Place in a dish, sprinkle with the vinegar, and cover thoroughly with several twists of black pepper. Leave to macerate in the fridge, covered, for half an hour, then add the brown sugar. Mix well, and then bind with the crême fraîche.

1 pint (550 ml) dry sherry
3 garlic cloves, peeled
3 green chillis
1 tsp black pepper
1 tsp horseradish, grated
Generous pinch celery seeds
Tomato juice
Vodka
Ice
Slices of lemon

Pour the sherry into a large jar, adding the garlic, chillis, pepper, horseradish and celery seeds. Leave for at least 24 hours, and then add a few drops to a glass of tomato juice and vodka (amounts according to taste). Add plenty of ice and decorate with a slice of lemon.